AUDIO ACCESS INCLUDED
Recorded Piano Accompaniments Online

PLAYBACK+
Speed • Pitch • Balance • Loop

SINGER'S JAZZ ANTHOLOGY | LOW VOICE

cole porter

Arranged by Brent Edstrom

T0081891

Cover photo © Getty Images / Hulton Deutsch / Contributor

To access audio visit:
www.halleonard.com/mylibrary

Enter Code
5380-3637-0324-4369

ISBN 978-1-5400-4199-9

HAL•LEONARD®

Visit Hal Leonard Online at
www.halleonard.com

Contact us:
Hal Leonard
7777 West Bluemound Road
Milwaukee, WI 53213
Email: info@halleonard.com

In Europe, contact:
Hal Leonard Europe Limited
42 Wigmore Street
Marylebone, London, W1U 2RN
Email: info@halleonardeurope.com

In Australia, contact:
Hal Leonard Australia Pty. Ltd.
4 Lentara Court
Cheltenham, Victoria, 3192 Australia
Email: info@halleonard.com.au

ARRANGER'S NOTE

The vocalist's part in the *Singer's Jazz Anthology* matches the original sheet music but is *not* intended to be sung verbatim. Instead, melodic embellishments and alterations of rhythm and phrasing should be incorporated to both personalize a performance and conform to the accompaniments. In some cases, the form has been expanded to include "tags" and other endings not found in the original sheet music. In these instances, the term *ad lib.* indicates new melodic material appended to the original form.

Although the concept of personalizing rhythms and embellishing melodies might seem awkward to singers who specialize in classical music, there is a long tradition of melodic variation within the context of performance dating back to the Baroque. Not only do jazz singers personalize a given melody to fit the style of an accompaniment, they also develop a distinctive sound that helps *further* personalize their performances. Undoubtedly, the best strategy for learning how to stylize a jazz melody is to listen to recordings from the vocal jazz canon, including artists such as Nat King Cole, Ella Fitzgerald, Billie Holiday, Frank Sinatra, Sarah Vaughan, Nancy Wilson, and others.

The accompaniments in the *Singer's Jazz Anthology* can also be embellished by personalizing rhythms or dynamics, and chord labels are provided for pianists who are comfortable playing their own chord voicings. In some cases, optional, written-out improvisations are provided. These can be performed "as is," embellished, or skipped, depending on the performers' preference.

The included audio features piano recordings that can be used as a rehearsal aid or to accompany a performance. Tempi were selected to fit the character of each accompaniment, and the optional piano solos were omitted to provide a more seamless singing experience for vocalists who utilize them as backing tracks.

I hope you find many hours of enjoyment exploring the *Singer's Jazz Anthology* series!

Brent Edstrom

BEGIN THE BEGUINE

from JUBILEE

Words and Music by
COLE PORTER

Moderate Swing

When they be-gin _____ the Be-guine, _____ it

brings back the sound _____ of mu-sic so ten-der. _____ It

brings back a night _____ of trop-i-cal splen-dor, _____ it

ALL OF YOU
from SILK STOCKINGS

Words and Music by
COLE PORTER

ANYTHING GOES

from ANYTHING GOES

Words and Music by
COLE PORTER

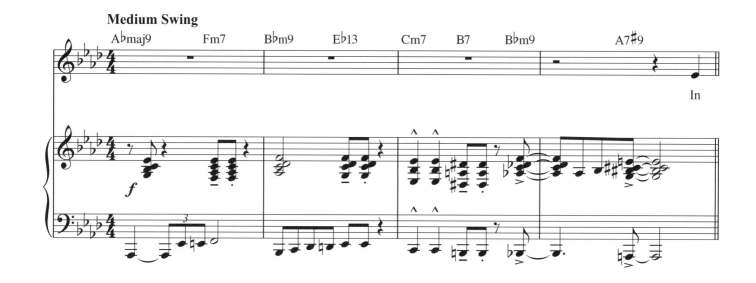

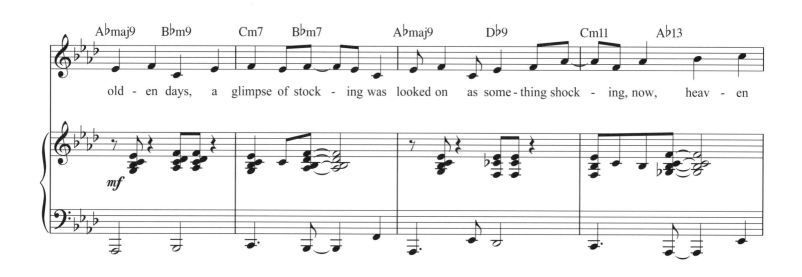

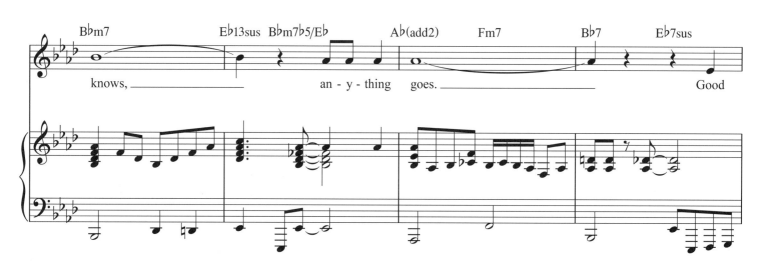

AT LONG LAST LOVE

from YOU NEVER KNOW

Words and Music by
COLE PORTER

Lyrics:

I'm so in love, and though it
gives me joy in-tense, I can't de-ci-pher, if I'm a
lif - er or if it's just a first of - fense.

EASY TO LOVE
(You'd Be So Easy to Love)
from BORN TO DANCE

Words and Music by
COLE PORTER

GET OUT OF TOWN

from LEAVE IT TO ME

Words and Music by
COLE PORTER

no - where you come to me as be - fore. To take my heart and

break my heart once more. _____

Bright Swing

Get out of town ____ Be - fore ____ it's too late, my love; _____

____ Get out of town, ____ Be good ____ to me, please. _____

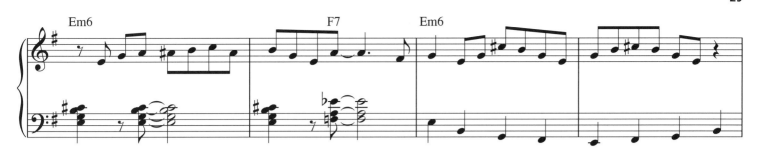

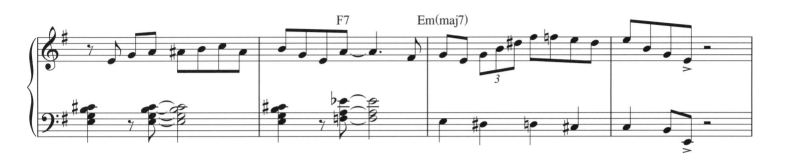

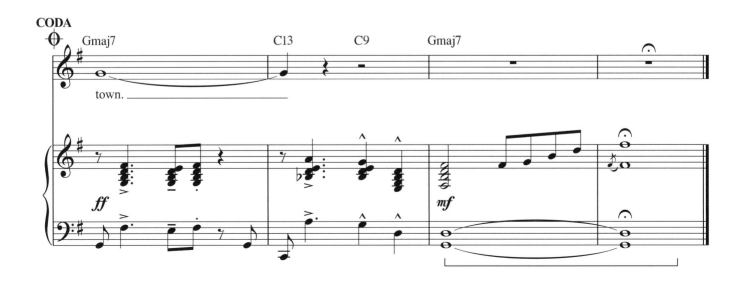

EV'RY TIME WE SAY GOODBYE

from SEVEN LIVELY ARTS

Words and Music by
COLE PORTER

FROM THIS MOMENT ON
from OUT OF THIS WORLD

Words and Music by
COLE PORTER

I CONCENTRATE ON YOU

from BROADWAY MELODY OF 1940

Words and Music by
COLE PORTER

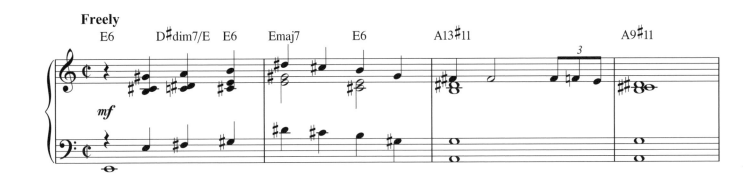

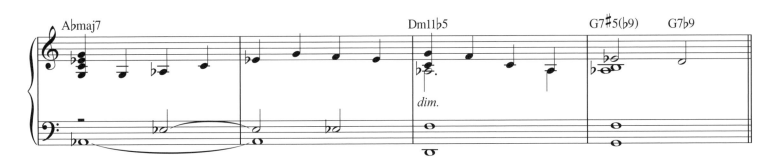

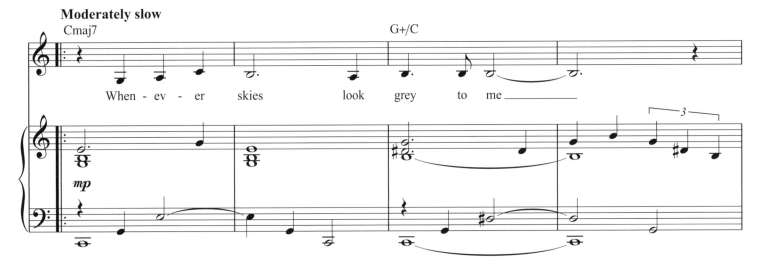

When-ev-er skies look grey to me

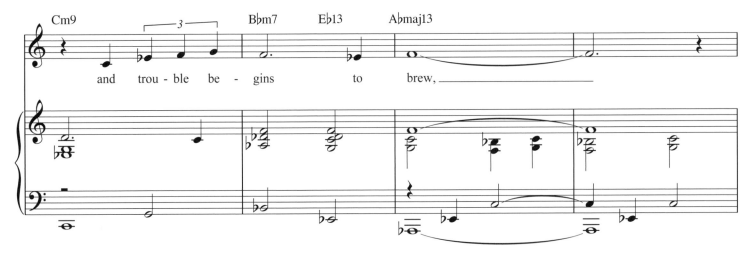

and trou-ble be-gins to brew,

I'VE GOT YOU UNDER MY SKIN

from BORN TO DANCE

Words and Music by
COLE PORTER

I GET A KICK OUT OF YOU

from ANYTHING GOES

Words and Music by
COLE PORTER

I LOVE PARIS
from CAN-CAN

Words and Music by
COLE PORTER

IN THE STILL OF THE NIGHT

from ROSALIE

Words and Music by
COLE PORTER

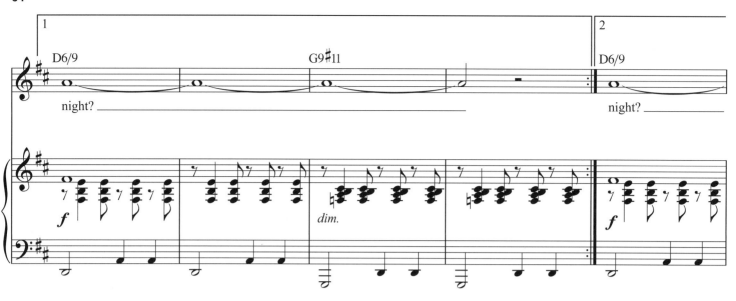

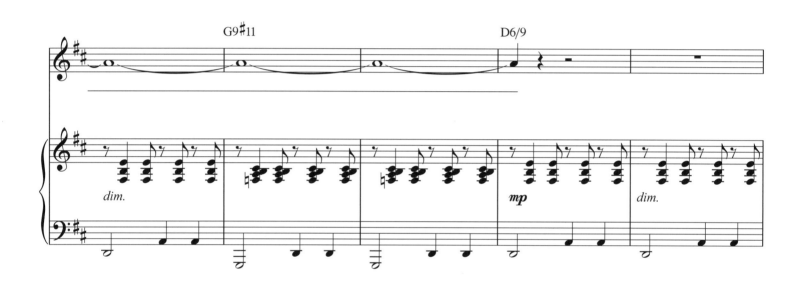

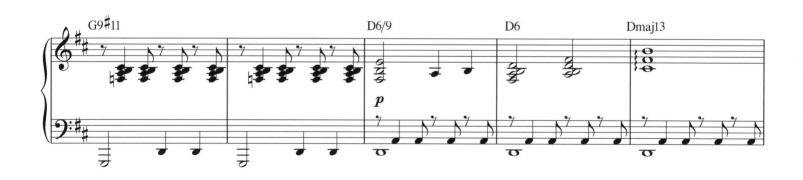

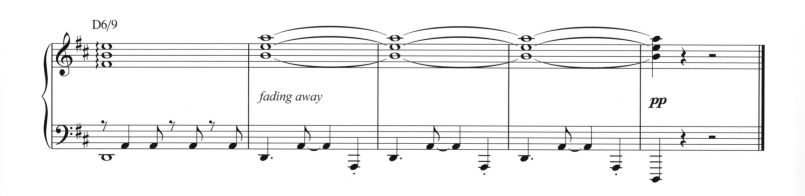

IT'S ALL RIGHT WITH ME

from CAN-CAN

Words and Music by
COLE PORTER

IT'S DE-LOVELY

from RED, HOT AND BLUE!

Words and Music by
COLE PORTER

JUST ONE OF THOSE THINGS

from HIGH SOCIETY

Words and Music by
COLE PORTER

LET'S DO IT
(Let's Fall in Love)
from PARIS

Words and Music by
COLE PORTER

LOVE FOR SALE

from THE NEW YORKERS

Words and Music by
COLE PORTER

NIGHT AND DAY
from GAY DIVORCE

Words and Music by
COLE PORTER

RIDIN' HIGH

from RED, HOT AND BLUE!

Words and Music by
COLE PORTER

TOO DARN HOT
from KISS ME, KATE

Words and Music by
COLE PORTER

WHAT IS THIS THING CALLED LOVE?

from WAKE UP AND DREAM

Words and Music by
COLE PORTER

YOU'D BE SO NICE TO COME HOME TO

from SOMETHING TO SHOUT ABOUT

Words and Music by
COLE PORTER

YOU'RE THE TOP

from ANYTHING GOES

Words and Music by
COLE PORTER

YOU DO SOMETHING TO ME

from CAN-CAN

Words and Music by
COLE PORTER